Favorite Books

My Book Lending Library

Created by AG Randall

ISBN-13: 978-1494904821
ISBN-10: 1494904829

First Printing, 2014

Printed in the United States of America

Favorite Books

Book Title	Author	Returned	Borrower

Favorite Books

Book Title	Author	Returned	Borrower

Favorite Books

Book Title	Author	Returned	Borrower

Favorite Books

Book Title	Author	Returned	Borrower

Favorite Books

Book Title	Author	Returned	Borrower

Favorite Books

Book Title	Author	Returned	Borrower

Favorite Books

Book Title	Author	Returned	Borrower

Favorite Books

Book Title	Author	Returned	Borrower

Favorite Books

Book Title	Author	Returned	Borrower

Favorite Books

Book Title	Author	Returned	Borrower

Favorite Books

Book Title	Author	Returned	Borrower

Favorite Books

Book Title	Author	Returned	Borrower

Favorite Books

Book Title	Author	Returned	Borrower

Favorite Books

Book Title	Author	Returned	Borrower

Favorite Books

Book Title	Author	Returned	Borrower

Favorite Books

Book Title	Author	Returned	Borrower

Favorite Books

Book Title	Author	Returned	Borrower

Favorite Books

Book Title	Author	Returned	Borrower

Favorite Books

Book Title	Author	Returned	Borrower

Favorite Books

Book Title	Author	Returned	Borrower

Favorite Books

Book Title	Author	Returned	Borrower

Favorite Books

Book Title	Author	Returned	Borrower

Favorite Books

Book Title	Author	Returned	Borrower

Favorite Books

Book Title	Author	Returned	Borrower

Favorite Books

Book Title	Author	Returned	Borrower

Favorite Books

Book Title	Author	Returned	Borrower

Favorite Books

Book Title	Author	Returned	Borrower

Favorite Books

Book Title	Author	Returned	Borrower

Favorite Books

Book Title	Author	Returned	Borrower

Favorite Books

Book Title	Author	Returned	Borrower

Favorite Books

Book Title	Author	Returned	Borrower

Favorite Books

Book Title	Author	Returned	Borrower

Favorite Books

Book Title	Author	Returned	Borrower

Favorite Books

Book Title	Author	Returned	Borrower

Favorite Books

Book Title	Author	Returned	Borrower

Favorite Books

Book Title	Author	Returned	Borrower

Favorite Books

Book Title	Author	Returned	Borrower

Favorite Books

Book Title	Author	Returned	Borrower

Favorite Books

Book Title	Author	Returned	Borrower

Favorite Books

Book Title	Author	Returned	Borrower

Favorite Books

Book Title	Author	Returned	Borrower

Favorite Books

Book Title	Author	Returned	Borrower

Favorite Books

Book Title	Author	Returned	Borrower

Favorite Books

Book Title	Author	Returned	Borrower

Favorite Books

Book Title	Author	Returned	Borrower

Favorite Books

Book Title	Author	Returned	Borrower

Favorite Books

Book Title	Author	Returned	Borrower

Favorite Books

Book Title	Author	Returned	Borrower

Favorite Books

Book Title	Author	Returned	Borrower

Favorite Books

Book Title	Author	Returned	Borrower

Favorite Books

Book Title	Author	Returned	Borrower

Favorite Books

Book Title	Author	Returned	Borrower

Favorite Books

Book Title	Author	Returned	Borrower

Favorite Books

Book Title	Author	Returned	Borrower

Favorite Books

Book Title	Author	Returned	Borrower

Favorite Books

Book Title	Author	Returned	Borrower

Favorite Books

Book Title	Author	Returned	Borrower

Favorite Books

Book Title	Author	Returned	Borrower

Favorite Books

Book Title	Author	Returned	Borrower

Favorite Books

Book Title	Author	Returned	Borrower

Favorite Books

Book Title	Author	Returned	Borrower

Favorite Books

Book Title	Author	Returned	Borrower

Favorite Books

Book Title	Author	Returned	Borrower

Favorite Books

Book Title	Author	Returned	Borrower

Favorite Books

Book Title	Author	Returned	Borrower

Favorite Books

Book Title	Author	Returned	Borrower